T0319208

In Defence of Press Freedom in Africa:
An Essay

Tatah Mentan

Langaa Research & Publishing CIG
Mankon, Bamenda

Publisher:
Langaa RPCIG
Langaa Research & Publishing Common Initiative Group
P.O. Box 902 Mankon
Bamenda
North West Region
Cameroon
Langaagrp@gmail.com
www.langaa-rpcig.net

Distributed in and outside N. America by African Books Collective
orders@africanbookscollective.com
www.africanbookscollective.com

ISBN: 9956-762-86-5

DISCLAIMER
All views expressed in this publication are those of the author and do
not necessarily reflect the views of Langaa RPCIG.

Dedication

To those toiling and moiling for the liberation and democratization of the free press in Africa.

Table of Contents

Foreword

When Dr. Tatah Mentan requested me to write the foreword to this work, I considered it a singular privilege from someone whom I have always looked up to as a mentor in journalism, a model of scholarship, an adviser and indeed a 'grand frère' as the Francophone would say.

I first met Tatah Mentan in 1965 as a secondary school freshman (a 'fox'-- in Cameroon Protestant College campus lingo). He was a senior student at the time and ever since our paths have at one time or another crossed and separated with the vicissitude of time. When he passed the competitive exam into the Yaoundé International Higher School of Journalism (ESIJY) in 1972, he convinced me to do same the following year.

We later worked together in the national station of Radio Cameroon, Yaoundé during which he came up with the innovative idea of me and him doing the prime time evening newscast with me as anchor and him as news commentator. One had to be exceptionally knowledgeable and intellectually resourceful to produce a news commentary every working day of the week for several months. What Tatah Mentan was doing was not the banal personal reflections on general social matters some commentators are fond of boring their listeners with these days but solid, razor-edged analysis based on the news of the day. Thus at the end of each news cast, I usually introduced him referring to an item of the news presented: "As you heard in the news...." We were actually adapting what Walter Cronkite (anchor) and Eric Severide (Commentator) of the CBS TV fame were doing in the US in the mid- 70s. It was one of the exciting periods of my career and the audience always looked forward to this fresh new way of serving the news every evening of the greater part of 1978 and part of 1979 after which 'Spicerman' bolted off to the University of Nsukka, Nigeria for further studies. His quest for knowledge was and still is unquenchable. Even though both of us had been hinted about forthcoming appointments as assistant chiefs of service, he could not to be distracted from his goal.

Back in Cameroon by the mid-1980s and armed with a Ph.D. in Political Sociology, Dr. T naturally integrated into the Advanced School of Mass Communication (ASMAC former ESIJY) and thus began his career as an academic. In 1987, fate led me to ASMAC where I had been seconded as an adjunct lecturer and where I again met my old comrade-in-arms. There again we tried to bring some fresh air to the stale curriculum and did our best to mould one of the best crops of journalism professionals of English expression in Cameroon. Even when I fell out with the Director of the School over the question of alleged bribery by certain candidates to enter the school, Dr. T and I remained inseparable. We lived in the same neighbourhood in Yaoundé and spent many memorable evenings together analysing Cameroon's faulty steps on the road to democracy in the wake of the eastern wind of change in the early 1990s. While political parties mushroomed by the dozen every day, the pace of institutional change merely marked time as the regime perfected its electoral rigging machinery and tinkered with constitutional reform.

So when Dr. T decides to revisit some of his old scripts concerning freedom of the press, it is only because the issue is so close to his heart and one only needs to take a look at the headlines to realize that the war for freedom of the press is far from being won.

A casual look at reports by the Committee to Protect

Journalists (CPJ) clearly indicates that freedom of the press cannot be taken for granted; in fact the press has increasingly come under threat even more so under the canopy of the so-called 'liberal' political dispensation than during the authoritarian era.

Headlines reminiscent of the era of the Russian Gulag abound even in 2014: "Military Tribunal bars two journalists from practicing until further notice" was an October 29 2014 headline in Cameroon. And one has to wonder what journalism offense could warrant the jurisdiction of a military tribunal. "Two journalists accused of trying to overthrow the Biya regime". And when you get to the bottom of the matter, the journalists were merely being harassed for refusing to disclose the source of a letter in which the writer is purported to have declared that the Head of State was physically and politically unfit to govern. According to the regime's hangmen, the contents of the letter could spark unrest to the detriment of the security of the state. This state security bogey is increasingly being used a pretext for gagging the media.

Consider this rather scary headline of April 24 2014 on Cameroon: "The car of Denis Nkwebo, investigative journalist and editor of Le Jour private newspaper, exploded outside his house in Douala." He had been warned by acquaintances and contacts within government circles to be careful about his reporting on security forces. In the wake of Boko Haram terrorist atrocities in parts of northern Cameroon, the journalist had apparently discovered certain loopholes and inadequacies in the manner in which the army was conducting its operations and the army was not comfortable with that.

Still on Cameroon, the Bamenda-based independent Foundation Radio was closed in April 2013 for broadcasting an interview the authorities said incited secession. That same year, the National Communication Council banned 5 broadcast programmes and jailed the journalists on charges of defamation.

From neighbouring Nigeria, the story is not different, even worse as journalists increasingly face threats from non-state actors. In April 2012 we read headlines such as: "Bomb blast in This Day newsroom in Abuja by Boko Haram. Five dead and several injured." In fact it was one of three simultaneous bombings targeting three newspaper offices in Abuja and Kaduna.

One of the most potent modern threats against journalists is the rise of extremist groups who deliberately target journalists, writes Human Rights Watch Director Peter Bouckaert. This new phenomenon is becoming frequent in countries like Mali, DR Congo, Somalia and Nigeria.

According to Reporters without Borders, the war on terror is being exploited by governments that are quick to treat journalists as threats to national security. After the terrorist attack on the Westgate shopping Centre in Nairobi, there was a general call for unity behind leaders and security forces, but as awkward questions about government missteps emerged, the Interior Minister accused the press of not being patriotic. This same accusation was levelled against journalists criticizing government's handling of operations against Boko Haram in Nigeria and Cameroon.

Non state groups constitute the main source of danger for journalists in a number of countries such as militias in Libya, Al Shabab in Somalia and M23 in DR Congo who regard journalists as enemies.

CPJ says digital surveillance, unchecked murder of journalists and indirect commercial and political pressure are the three primary threats to freedom of the press. In 2013, it discloses, 70 journalists lost their lives in Egypt and Iraq. In DR Congo, at least 10 radio and TV stations were silenced for weeks and months at a time by government regulators and local officials and presenters suspended for airing programmes critical of government.

According to CPJ, there were 69 anti- press attacks in DR Congo alone in 2012 including threats, physical attacks, arbitrary detention, closures of news outlets, suspension of programmes and imprisonment.

In early November 2014 we learn that a Sierra Leone journalist of the Citizen FM radio had been imprisoned for criticizing President Bai Koroma's handling of the Ebola outbreak. The journalist is said to have interviewed an opposition party spokesman who criticized President Koroma and his government's handling of the Ebola crisis and Koroma's intention to run for a third term in office.

Besides violent threats, indirect commercial and political pressure, another source of threat against freedom of the press paradoxically comes from the legal domain. After doing away with prior censorship that was the modus operandi under erstwhile authoritarian regimes, the post 1989 so-called plural and liberal regimes that emerged in Africa have resorted to the criminalization of defamation and an outright refusal to acknowledge and endorse the right of citizens to information. The fight for press freedom must focus on these two battlefronts with greater prospects of success if it can carry the public along.

Given all of the above, it is clear that press freedom is crying to be defended from power hungry politicians, overzealous administrators and regulatory boards seeking reward from their paymasters, incompetent security forces, religious fanatics and all those with skeletons in their cupboards.

By revisiting the issue of press freedom, Tatah Mentan is once more bringing to the forefront an issue society must deal with on a daily basis and urgently too. The relevance of the matter cannot be gainsaid and it is up to the press corps and their natural allies to take cognizance of the fact that it incumbent on them and no one else to stand at the frontline of the battle for press freedom.

Sam-Nuvala Fonkem,
United Nations Mission,
Abidjan, Côte d'Ivoire, 2014

Preface

The press has played an important role in Africa's tortuous transition to independence and democracy. Several news companies defied the tradition of media systems tamed and controlled by authoritarian regimes, and tried a new kind of journalism, more attuned with an open and democratic environment. It is impossible to generalize the direct or indirect role of the media in the entire continent since countries and political processes are very different from one another. There were, however, striking common traits among several newspapers that elbowed their ways to democracy amid hostile political environments.

The press had leading roles in their countries' endeavours to get out of the kind of dictatorships or authoritarian regimes that characterized Africa's contemporary history. They were surfing the crest of the wave of democratization that swept through the hemisphere. For the first time ever, Africa is almost totally ruled by elected governments. In some countries, this is the very first time in history that citizens have experienced a formal democracy. In others, democratic regimes were, historically, only brief intervals between dictatorships. At this time, the "interval" has lasted longer than ever, sparking strong hope that there is finally a chance for democratic systems to mature and be in place for good. There is, however, a long and difficult way to go before this happens.

Democracy is clearly under construction, and subject to threats of very strong antidemocratic forces firmly consolidated during most of the history of these nations. All over Africa, democratization comes together with economic reforms aiming to strengthen capitalism, the so-called neoliberal economic policies. In countries such as Ghana and South Africa, the economic reforms occurred before political openness. *New York Times* columnist Thomas L. Friedman noted that, "With the collapse of communism", every country now has the same "hardware." That is, they have all adopted free-market capitalism to one degree or another. But where they differ in the "software" – the institutions of the governance, be they regulatory bodies, a watchdog press, or uncorrupted courts, civil services, parliaments and police. Those that don't get the software right will become "free-market kleptocracies". This is a very accurate description that fits not only Africa and Latin America but also the newly democratized Eastern European countries, despite their huge difference from each other.

Given the widespread corruption in Africa and the result of investigative reporting in the cases we analyse here, the expression "kleptocracy" is an appropriate definition of certain political systems in the continent. Jeffrey Garten, Dean of Yale University's School of Management, was quoted as saying that, "After the Cold War, the assumption was that the countries which adopted the hardware of democratic capitalism, would inevitably develop the software. But adopting the hardware is the easiest part because there's no credible alternative model in the world today." He describes the "truly explosive problems" of "the transition from a system with no democratic tradition to a full-fledged democracy," that usually takes place at the same time of the transition "from a closed economy to an open one." These "two sets of forces, combined with the growing pressures of trade and technology, represent a frontal threat to a society's ability to govern itself."

In fact, the free press emerges as the most dynamic and often the most developed part of that software throughout

Africa. In tune with the democratization process, media outlets have changed substantially their role in society. From being tame government mouthpieces, the media have moved to an autonomous political position, in an evident effort to play the watchdog role reserved for them in a classic democratic system.

Many newspapers and journalists are trying to learn how to play that role, overcoming their own solid tradition of self-censorship and government dependence. One can easily posit that the issue is how to overcome "the culture of fear." This stemmed from decades of censorship imposed by dictators and from selfish oligarchs or elite members who owned media companies, using them for their benefit, without any social concern. The consequence was a series of restraints - including violence - on the practice of independent journalism, making Africa in cases as Sierra Leone and Zimbabwe in recent years one of the most dangerous places in the world for journalists.

During the dictatorships of the recent past, newspapers occasionally tested the limits imposed by the authorities and defied the rules. Governments often responded with violence, suspicious lawsuits against journalists and publishers, and economic boycotts against media companies. One of the most important consequences for the media of the recent free-market oriented economic reforms in Africa generally has been a substantial change in their relationship with the governments. Through a wave of privatization, the state's share of the economy is shrinking, as well as its capacity to buy advertisements. State or state-owned companies' paid ads have been one of the most effective forms of muzzling the press in the continent, but that is changing fast. At the same time, media companies are becoming so rich that an occasional government economic boycott against them would have very little effect. Therefore, instead of sticking with its comfortable tradition of supporting whoever is in the government, those companies have started searching for their watchdog role, which fits better with the new hardware, the free-market economy, and with the necessary software, the democratic system.

The consequences of that shift are seen elsewhere in the hemisphere, translated into exposes of malfeasance or human rights abuses investigated and printed by newspapers that just a few years ago would never have been interested in such controversial subjects. Historic cases, such as the ridiculing of presidents and the shift of some media outlets to a watchdog role, have caused the prestige of the press to skyrocket throughout the hemisphere. The downside has been, in some cases, a journalism hangover similar to the trend observed in the 1970s in the United States as a consequence of Watergate. In the American hangover, reporters all over the country tried to replicate the sensational performance of Woodward and Bernstein in the investigation that drove President Nixon to resign. The result was often an exaggerated effort to find new scandals every day. In Africa, democracy's hangover has had even worse consequences for journalism. Since institutions in nascent democracies are frequently weak, inefficient or ineffective, some journalists seem to believe that the media can substitute for the police, judiciary, or congress. This is obviously a mistake. Reputations have been killed by ill-investigated or one-sided stories, in an environment of fierce competition and poor journalistic education and skills. In cases like these, watchdog efforts backfire, damaging the media's prestige and provoking reactions that could have a negative effect on nascent democracies. Many newly democratized countries had waves of complaints about the alleged excesses of the press. Meanwhile, in some countries legislators filed bills to try to impose limits on journalistic work and inflict severe punishments on journalists and media companies.

However, the complaints about exaggerated reporting in Africa are not always justified. On the contrary, it is much more common for governments to consider abusive what is legitimate criticism or journalistic probing. In certain, the democracy's vanguard newspapers had in common precisely this kind of sound antagonism toward authorities not accustomed to a watchdog press. Those daily papers played a very important role in opposing and resisting authoritarian regimes. They have acted as spearheads of democratic forces, openly defying oppressive political systems and even other media outlets that have been tamed or in mutually beneficial collusion with governments. Perhaps their most important common trait is that the newspapers set an example for the rest of the media, strongly influencing them to change their editorial lines and reporting styles, to adapt themselves to the new times of political openness and democracy.

In most cases, the endeavour has been very successful from a business point of view as well as the political and editorial perspectives. Some newspapers showed the others it was possible to run a newspaper committed to democracy and independence from the government, and make it a profitable operation. In other cases, the papers that played this important political role during democratization could not achieve that same business success. The failure could be attributed to fierce competition or to their own inability to overcome economic problems (politically originated or not).

Many of the reforms, shake-ups, and revelations of scandals of the past several decades of misrule, repression, mismanagement, kleptocracy, state terrorism and genocide in Africa originated not in a legislator's office or diligent regulatory committee but in a daily paper's newsroom. This is indicative of why, within the government, more energy is devoted in a single day to feeding and fending off the press than it takes either to plan a coup d'état or draft a constitution.

As African governments become sensitive and cautious when confronted by the press, the universe of frank and open news reporting is restricted, and honest and thorough –going dialogue becomes more difficult.

Yet, the major problems facing Africa today are how to (1) forge virile and united countries out of the conglomeration of ethnic groups and classes united only by their eventual mutual collision; (2) develop the underdeveloped neo-colonial economies rapidly, in order to give the "wretched." masses a decent standard of living and thus satisfy their legitimate expectations; (3) build democratic structures of free and competitive political parties and banish the rule by decree of politicians in uniform, Western suits, and in "agbada"; (4) establish faire and regular electoral processes with strict adherence to rules which regulate elections; (5) nurture an electorate insulated from intimidations and prompting which emasculate the exercise of free will; (6) groom elected representatives of the people who make laws on behalf and in the interest of those they represent; and (7) operate a judiciary that must be an unfettered purveyor of justice and equity as well as a custodian of basic freedoms.

Most African governments doubtfully tackle these issues as priorities. Rather, unanimity has been the absolute political value. The notion of public welfare, of civic spirit, of a job well done have become hazy, and are ending up being obliterated by the personal self-interests of ossified political oligarchies - military or civilian. The normal reaction of these oligarchies has been to promote rife immorality since they are architects of Africa bedevilled by Lexis, clienteles, generalised corruption, political gangsterism and "kleptocratic tribalocracy".

This, perhaps, explains why the normal reaction of the concerned African press has been to oppose such wanton but systematic repression of opposition groups, intimidation of their activities and electoral fraud. After all, is it not easier for a government to curtain off its mistakes of political orientation, economic choice and national resource management by torturing and jailing a few journalists?

This commonplace action of torturing, killing, and jailing "dissenting journalists" by anti-people African regimes compels a spirited defence of press freedom in this continent as the only shield against social disequilibrium. It is for this reason that I wrote this essay, which has been gathering dust in my file for decades.

Tatah Mentan, Ph.D.
Minnesota, 2014

Principles of Journalism

The first year of our training in journalism involved listening and talking with our teacher, Mr. Sammy Chumfong. He concentrated on compelling us to understand what defined the work of a journalist. *Bourgeois*, as we referred to him in our private conversations, apparently nursed the fear that we could get lost in the profession, if we were not well groomed or threw the professional principles of journalism outside with the bathwater to obtain juicy political appointments. One could read from his unwavering gentle emphasis that he feared betrayal by students (Richard Nyamboli, Zachary Nkwo and Tatah Mentan) who may be armed with professional ignorance as his products. To him, this ignorance would soil his professional reputation as a teacher and professional journalist. This was in 1973. I wrote the framework for this Essay in 1974. Whether we have ruined Mr. Chumfong's image as his professional products is for history to judge. However, what emerged out of Mr. Chumfong's lectures and conversations with the three of us were built around the following nine core principles of professional journalism that I carried along with me until I jumped into a different field of study (See Appendix for elaboration):

1. Journalism's first obligation is to the truth

Democracy depends on citizens having reliable, accurate facts put in a meaningful context. Journalism does not pursue truth in an absolute or philosophical sense, but it can–and must–pursue it in a practical sense. This "journalistic truth" is a process that begins with the professional discipline of assembling and verifying facts. Then journalists try to convey a fair and reliable account of their meaning, valid for now, subject to further investigation. Journalists should be as transparent as possible about sources and methods so audiences can make their own assessment of the information. Even in a world of expanding voices, accuracy is the foundation upon which everything else is built–context, interpretation, comment, criticism, analysis and debate. The truth, over time, emerges from this forum. As citizens encounter an ever greater flow of data, they have more need– not less–for identifiable sources dedicated to verifying that information and putting it in context.

2. Its first loyalty is to citizens

While news organizations answer to many constituencies, including advertisers and shareholders, the journalists in those organizations must maintain allegiance to citizens and the larger public interest above any other if they are to provide the news without fear or favour. This commitment to citizens first is the basis of a news organization's credibility, the implied covenant that tells the audience the coverage is not slanted for friends or advertisers. Commitment to citizens also means journalism should present a representative picture of all constituent groups in society. Ignoring certain citizens has the effect of disenfranchising them. The theory underlying the modern news industry has been the belief that credibility builds a broad and loyal audience, and that economic success follows in turn. In that regard, the business people in a news organization also must nurture – not exploit – their allegiance to the audience ahead of other considerations.

3. Its essence is a discipline of verification

Journalists rely on a professional discipline for verifying

information. When the concept of objectivity originally evolved, it did not imply that journalists are free of bias. It called, rather, for a consistent method of testing information– a transparent approach to evidence–precisely so that personal and cultural biases would not undermine the accuracy of their work. The method is objective, not the journalist. Seeking out multiple witnesses, disclosing as much as possible about sources, or asking various sides for comment, all signal such standards. This discipline of verification is what separates journalism from other modes of communication, such as propaganda, fiction or entertainment. But the need for professional method is not always fully recognized or refined. While journalism has developed various techniques for determining facts, for instance, it has done less to develop a system for testing the reliability of journalistic interpretation.

4. Its practitioners must maintain an independence from those they cover

Independence is an underlying requirement of journalism, a cornerstone of its reliability. Independence of spirit and mind, rather than neutrality, is the principle journalists must keep in focus. While editorialists and commentators are not neutral, the source of their credibility is still their accuracy, intellectual fairness and ability to inform–not their devotion to a certain group or outcome. In our independence, however, we must avoid any tendency to stray into arrogance, elitism, isolation or nihilism.

5. It must serve as an independent monitor of power

Journalism has an unusual capacity to serve as watchdog over those whose power and position most affect citizens. The Founders recognized this to be a rampart against despotism when they ensured an independent press; courts have affirmed it; citizens rely on it. As journalists, we have an obligation to protect this watchdog freedom by not demeaning it in frivolous use or exploiting it for commercial gain.

6. It must provide a forum for public criticism and compromise

The news media are the common carriers of public discussion, and this responsibility forms a basis for our special privileges. This discussion serves society best when it is informed by facts rather than prejudice and supposition. It also should strive to fairly represent the varied viewpoints and interests in society, and to place them in context rather than highlight only the conflicting fringes of debate. Accuracy and truthfulness require that as framers of the public discussion we not neglect the points of common ground where problem solving occurs.

7. It must strive to make the significant interesting and relevant

Journalism is storytelling with a purpose. It should do more than gather an audience or catalogue the important. For its own survival, it must balance what readers know they want with what they cannot anticipate but need. In short, it must strive to make the significant interesting and relevant. The effectiveness of a piece of journalism is measured both by how much a work engages its audience and enlightens it. This means journalists must continually ask what information has most value to citizens and in what form. While journalism should reach beyond such topics as government and public safety, a journalism overwhelmed by trivia and false significance ultimately engenders a trivial society.

8. It must keep the news comprehensive and proportional

Keeping news in proportion and not leaving important things out are also cornerstones of truthfulness. Journalism is a form of cartography: it creates a map for citizens to navigate society. Inflating events for sensation, neglecting others, stereotyping or being disproportionately negative all make a less reliable map. The map also should include news of all our communities, not just those with attractive demographics. This is best achieved by newsrooms with a diversity of backgrounds and perspectives. The map is only an analogy; proportion and comprehensiveness are subjective, yet their elusiveness does not lessen their significance.

9. Its practitioners must be allowed to exercise their personal conscience

Every journalist must have a personal sense of ethics and responsibility—a moral compass. Each of us must be willing, if fairness and accuracy require, to voice differences with our colleagues, whether in the newsroom or the executive suite. News organizations do well to nurture this independence by encouraging individuals to speak their minds. This stimulates the intellectual diversity necessary to understand and accurately cover an increasingly diverse society. It is this diversity of minds and voices, not just numbers that matters.

During this period, the following distinctive and enduring elements of the African political systems emerged:

o a one-party system in which the Single Party controlled decisions having to do with political appointments, economic policy, cultural activities, and foreign relations;

o a personal dictatorship in which loyalty to a single leader, the President, had to be unquestioned and the image of the omnipotent leader filled public discourse;

o a pervasive system of police controls, forced labour, and violent repression that killed millions, imprisoned even more, and imposed restrictions on any kind of public speech, assembly, or organization;

o a system of forced import-substitution "modernization" that transformed small-scale agriculture into state-run farms and rapidly expanded wasteful, dependent, and clientelist industrial production by building factories, expanding mining, and developing transportation for economic extraversion; and

o a foreign policy that sought to protect national borders and a personalist ideology through a combination of military power, as in the Soviet victory over Nazi Germany during World War II, and expanding protective borders by establishing loyal regimes in neo-colonial frameworks.

Propaganda and Censorship

Once the African regimes succeeded in ending Western-style electoral democracy and turning the continent into a one-party or military dictatorships, they orchestrated a massive propaganda campaign to win the loyalty and cooperation of citizens in the name of national security. The propaganda ministries took control of all forms of communication: newspapers, magazines, books, public meetings, and rallies, art, music, movies, and radio. Viewpoints in any way threatening to the President's beliefs or to the regime were censored or eliminated from all media. Student organizations, professors, and librarians made up long lists of books they thought should not be read. The censors also burned the books of authors who espoused the maxim that: "Tyranny cannot defeat the power of ideas.

Schools also played an important role in spreading Nazi ideas. While some books were removed from classrooms by censors, other textbooks, newly written, were brought in to teach students blind obedience to the party, love for the President. After-school meetings of One-Party Youth trained children to be faithful to the party. In school and out, young people celebrated such occasions as the anniversary of the President's taking power and the imposition of the single-party.

The increasing notoriety of regimes in their violent and militaristic approach to responding to contrary views and public debates was very scary. Under these African political systems of authoritarianism that predominated, the repressive features were meant to enable the leaders to retain a monopoly of power and, increasingly, to prevent a genuine opposition to threaten the elite's authority. Here are the principal instruments of control that existed and some have been perfected with the revolution in information technology:

Elections: The major goal was to mobilize the resources of the state to ensure the outcome of elections well before Election Day. This required tolerating weak or pliant opposition parties or even creating sham parties that made no effort at genuine competition. Potentially strong opposition leaders were dealt with through trumped up legal cases, with corruption charges the usual vehicle. Media coverage was not merely biased but intended to make opposition candidates seem buffoonish, extreme, or unpatriotic.

Media: Nothing was more critical to a successful authoritarian than control of the political message. Modern authoritarians do not use the old techniques of censorship. Instead, they gain control of the principal sources of news - often national television stations - through state ownership or ownership by the leader's cronies. Critical voices were excluded from the airwaves while the leadership's policies are given extensive, positive coverage.

Internet: For some time, the internet has become the major source of opposition perspectives. Recently, however, things have changed, as country after country has imposed controls on new media content, usually by blocking websites or blogs operated by the opposition, as the commonplace practice today.

Protests: With elections effectively rigged, the opposition has often taken their case to the streets through demonstrations and sometimes creative forms of street theatre. This weapon, however, has been put in jeopardy by laws which effectively make protests illegal. In some countries, protest leaders are being prosecuted for treason.

Universities: A traditional haven for freedom of thought, universities were increasingly finding themselves under pressure. Professors with dissenting views had been fired or coerced into toeing the line of the leader.

Civil Society: Civil society organizations were permitted to function normally as long as they avoided sensitive political issues. But non-governmental organizations that defended political prisoners, investigated cases of corruption, or monitor elections were eventually destroyed through tax prosecutions, libel suits, or bogus corruption accusations.

Judges: Politically charged legal cases were often decided through "telephone justice," whereby the judge would be instructed on the decision and sentence by a call from party officials. Political control of the judiciary was a core feature of African authoritarian regimes. While defendants in political cases occasionally avoided prison time, the fact that the prosecution occasionally "loses" a case reinforced the capricious and unpredictable nature of the system.

Increasingly, we are seeing a template for dictators being forged by the world's most durable despots. By ridding themselves of the stupidities, today's authoritarians may have created a system that is more part of the real world of trade and diplomacy, less identified with a foreign power, and therefore less vulnerable to outside pressure than was Soviet communism. While the gains that accompanied the end of the Cold War remain largely in place, democracy is today facing its most serious challenge of the past quarter-century. That is why this piece, drafted since two scores of years ago, is still relevant today.

A Statement of Concern

This is a critical moment for journalism in Africa. While the craft in many respects has never been better - considering the supply of information or the skills of reporters in the era of information technology-there is a paradox to our communications age. Revolutionary changes in technology, in our economic structure and in our relationship with the public, are pulling journalism from its traditional moorings.

As audiences fragment and companies diversify, there is a growing debate within news organizations about responsibilities as businesses versus responsibilities as journalism. Many journalists feel a sense of lost purpose. There is even doubt about the meaning of news, doubt evident when serious journalists organizations drift toward opinion, infotainment and sensation out of balance with news.

Journalists share responsibility for this uncertainty. Professional values and professional standards are often vaguely expressed and inconsistently honoured. We have been slow to change habits in the presentation of the news that may lose their relevance. Change is necessary.

Yet as we change we assert some core principles of journalism that are enduring. They are those that make journalism a public service critical to self-government. They define our profession not as the act of communicating but as a set of responsibilities. Journalism can entertain, amuse and lift our spirits, but news organizations also must cover the matters vital to the well- being of their increasingly diverse communities to foster the debate upon which democracy depends. Journalism implies obligation as well as freedom.

For much of our history, we believed we could let our work enunciate these principles and our owners and managers articulate these responsibilities. Today, too often, the principles in our work are hard to discern or lost in the din, and our leaders feel constrained.

Now we believe journalists must speak for themselves. We call on our colleagues to join as a community of professionals to clarify the purpose and principles that distinguish our profession from other forms of communications.

Since the change we face is fundamental, it requires a response of the same magnitude. We need a focused examination of the demands on African journalism of the 21st Century.

We propose to summon journalists to a period of national reflection. First, we ask our colleagues, young and old, to sign this declaration of concern. We believe the consortium of journalists who share a commitment to common principles is so broad and so significant that it will constitute a powerful movement toward renewal.

Next we will recommend the convening of sets of public forums around the continent over the next several months to hear the concerns of journalists as well as other interested individuals. The forums should reiterate two simple messages: that journalists of all generations are concerned about the direction of the profession; and that they want to clarify their purpose and principles. We do not presume to enumerate those principles here, but hope to have them articulated through the forums. These sessions will include the public. An interim reports after each one should be published. At their conclusion, the group will release a final report that will attempt to define the enduring purpose of journalism, along with its principles, responsibilities and aspirations.

We see this as a beginning, a catalyst forging new ideas and renewed spirit of conviction. We should all plan to carry the dialogue forward with a web site, videotapes of the forums and through other means. We do not intend to propose a set of solutions: this is an attempt to clarify our common ground. Nor is my motive to develop a detailed code of conduct. If journalism is a set of aims, how we fulfil them should change with changing times and be left to each news organization to decide. But if journalism is to survive, it falls to individual journalists, especially in each new generation, to articulate what it stands.

Indeed,

.... If a college doesn't teach a man to think his own thoughts and speak his own mind, it doesn't teach him anything of prime importance. Oh, he may accumulate any amount of book learning, he may be fluent in seventeen languages including the Etruscan, he may be able to square the circle... But if he comes out of college without the capacity to form an opinion of the way the world is going and the nerve to stand on that opinion in the face of stout opposition, he remains an ignoramus, though his degrees may take up half the letters of the alphabet.

(Gerald W. Johnson)

Chapter 1

The Media Context

"In order to function effectively as citizens the people must have access to the unfettered truth. Without this access, our whole foundation of government will crumble."
(Mark Hayfield)

Press Freedom - which has become a rather "pompous" and "hated" term for freedom of, and within the instruments of mass media of communication – is today under threat of extinction in several quarters in Africa, the noisiness about democracy notwithstanding. And it urgently needs to be defended. This need is surely not merely to defend what there is, but to extend "press freedom" into media institutions and other areas where it hardly exists at all - except as a hollow phrase, (on tiresome speech days, and the like) in which Africa's fossilized political systems celebrate their own conservatism.

Press freedom and political democracy are twins. And like so many words that are bandied about, the phrase "press freedom" threatens to become meaningless in Africa because it has become very banal. And banalization is an excellent device for drying up a truth by sponging upon it since the substance of the functional orientation of the case in point can easily become lost in a cloud of hazy definitions.

Threats to press derive from the authoritarian structures of African political institutions in which practitioners tend to rely on rule- of- thumb and institution. African states which constantly advertise themselves as "free and democratic"

1

manage to tolerate an extraordinary degree of authoritarianism within nearly all their major institutions. This contradiction between pretensions and practice is unlikely to last indefinitely. Sooner or later a compelling choice must be made between greater press freedom and democracy, or less. There are inviting signs that some African rulers have already made their obvious choice – for repression-without the rest of African humanity and the world having to decide whether to accept this or resist it. Go to Gabon and you will be shocked if you try to talk about media pluralism. It will be equated to "anti-Bongoism".

At the moment, in direct response to various forms of popular discontent about the failure of several African rulers to bring promised freedom to their people, the continent is becoming less free. The political systems are tightening up as they sing the virtues of democracy in order to qualify for western "aid", in hot pursuit of their endemic policies of repressively stealing at home and begging abroad. Press dissent, whether peaceable or not, becomes increasingly suspect and risky. The attempts, often successful, to brutalize "subversive" journalists as the "Amakiri affaire" in Nigeria or throw them with impunity behind bars like Idi Amin or simply kill them with letter bombs like the case of Dele Giwa in Nigeria form one element in this overall pattern. This is one reason why these cases have a more than local significance and why press freedom is something more than a privileged minority's vested interest. Repressive intolerance in the press freedom sphere is particularly ominous, just because it is so alien to the "official" ideologies of freedom of opinion on which press freedom is supposed to be founded. So if radicalism, or even non-political deviance, cannot be tolerated in the "press", it is unlikely to be very secure anywhere else. The fight for press freedom matters for humanistic reasons.

But it is also of concern to all libertarians - African and non-African.

Definition of Freedom

What is freedom, particularly press freedom and why does it matter? The phrase is one which commands almost universal routine assent. Every journalist, intellectual, military dictator or civilian politician pays verbal tribute to it. Not even the authoritarian of the *Right*, or those of the *Left* for whom "liberal" is normally a term of contempt, will disdain to invoke it when convenient. It would seem that "everyone" would be against sin. Perhaps, this familiarity with the work makes "everyone" grow a premature and apocalyptic belief in it.

But, as is so often the case, this superficial consensus conceals real and fundamental differences of opinion. It turns out, unfortunately, that freedom, as usual, is a work which everyone uses, but to mean quite different things. For those who still cling to the antiquated dogmas of laissez-faire, press freedom necessarily means freedom for the favourite bogey of the Right - state intervention. Others with rather similar tangential views equate press freedom quite narrowly with the freedom of journalists and therefore see the chief threat to freedom in mass demands for participation in criticizing the press and the government. This semantic chaos makes the press to lose its preordained place in Africa and collapse into deserved disuse.

Some have been quick to cry out in defiance of press freedom in their countries when journalists have been shouted down or even simply heckled, by foreign humanitarian agencies, but they have remained silent, or expressed open support, when radical or dissident journalists have been victimized or have lost their jobs - a much more serious penalty. Others, including ourselves, have on the contrary, seen in the intolerance and the unrestrained power of African publics, rulers and journalists the single greatest threat to press freedom today in this continent.

How are we to choose between these competing conceptions? We can do so without paying more detailed attention to the idea of freedom itself. Freedom is a concept that ought to provoke questions, not merely monotonous spontaneous assent, and the crucial questions are always — freedom for whom, in practice? And from what, to do what? General slogans invoking freedom have often been in practice a rhetorical camouflage for sectarian vested interests. For example, a "free" economy is always more free for some than others.

Freedom of the press, though apparently a straightforward notion, bristles with similar problems. Who exactly are "the press"? Is it freedom of journalists, or print workers, or editors, or owners of newspapers, that is being talked about? If editors have the freedom to refuse to print a reader's letter, or a journalist's report, what happens to the freedom of the unpublished writer? If reporters have the freedom to pursue news or "human interest" stories into people's homes and families, what happens to the freedom of the people whose privacy is so grossly violated? To some it is obvious that the print workers who occasionally object to printing certain cartoons or articles have been attempting to operate some censorship. But why should editors have the right to reject contributions, and not print workers? From these muffled questions, the question of whose freedom is being referred to is obscured rather than answered in a general phrase like "freedom of the press". The general slogan hangs on all lips that "freedom for the pike is death for the minnows". And freedom for the pike is not the same as freedom for all fish. As with other freedoms, therefore, we have to decide whose freedom is involved when we speak of press freedom, especially in "democratic systems" grown up by Africa's hydraulic regimes.

The close link between the conception of freedom and power is implicit in the pike/minnows proverbs : Where power is unequally distributed, and apparent general freedom is in practice only available to those with the power to make use of it : To say that the press is free because anyone is "free" to become a millionaire. The same holds at that other end of the economic spectrum. As Anatole France pointed out: "the rich as well as the poor are free to sleep under the bridges of Paris". Where specific freedoms are involved, it is clear that freedom for some will be power for others. And power for some necessarily implies powerlessness for others. Often it means worse than that – dependence, subservience and even oppression. To say that politicians, civil servants hand-picked into "responsible" posts and spineless journalists should be "free" to decide what the public should know is authoritarian, no matter how benevolently intended and exercised. Such a sanguine conviction is implicitly based on the sacrilegious and masochistic assumption that the people ordained with such extravagant power are omniscient and omnipotent.

In theory it is possible to envisage mass media institutions as benign despotisms in which a high degree of freedom is allowed to journalists and they publish what they like, with the key word being "allowed". Such voluntary renunciations of the exercise of power and authority are always unreliable. They are apt to be temporary, since they are dependent not on acknowledged right, but on the occasionally liberal character of the authorities concerned. Autocratic structures

5

co-exist uneasily with freedom for journalists and publics. In such circumstances freedom survives under perpetual threat of interference or abolition. So, any discussion of press freedom cannot avoid discussing how that freedom is and ought to be distributed among all those involved in communication; and that involves us in discussing the power structures of communication and media institutions.

Next, freedom is always freedom to do something. Here again the simple slogan "press freedom" leaves this question begged or unanswered: freedom to do what? Freedom from what? To these questions there is a short and relatively straightforward answer, which, however, can only be the beginning of a more complex discussion.

The freedom that matters is the openness of the channels of communication, that is, the tolerance of a great range and diversity of approaches and opinions, not only in relation to specific topics handled, but also in relation to journalism itself, its purposes and methods. This implies that journalists and the public should be free to put forward the interpretations which they believe in. In journalism the freedom to hold opinions, especially unorthodox opinions, and to advocate them openly and without any fear of reprisal, is supremely important. It has always been recognized, as a principle, that this openness requires that journalists should be appointed on the score of their competence and nothing else.

It is not the business of insensitive administrators and opportunistic politicians to set themselves up as arbiters of the politics or the morality of journalists – although they frequently do so. This is not because journalism has nothing to do with moral values or politics, or because journalists should not be concerned with the overall personal growth of those they try to inform. Quite the contrary! The role of values and of ideology in journalism cannot be denied. But it is because this is an area of irreducible disagreements that it is quite wrong, too wrong, to try to impose one particular set of moral, religious or political values as a test of journalistic acceptability. When this imposition occurs the media acquire some unfitness or trained incapacity.

But press freedom has other broader dimensions. Press freedom requires that diversity, flexibility and experiment should be, not merely grudgingly tolerated, but actively encouraged. It requires of the press itself a constant process of self-criticism, directed above all at the ideological orthodoxies which invariably play a large part in determining both what the society is and how it is steered. For communications does not, of course, stand outside society in this respect. Considering how little agreement there could be about either the purposes and methods of communications, or the interpretation of particular topics of interest to the society, it is astonishing how intolerant most media authorities are of unorthodoxy in these areas. An individual journalist, or a topic which does not conform to conventional authority or dominated patterns, all can only too easily fall foul of outraged respectability.

We have come close to a preliminary answer to some of the questions posed earlier. Press freedom and freedom in communications must first be for those directly involved in the process, as journalists and the public. The freedom that matters is the freedom to write and to speak according to one's convictions and interests. We have deliberately stressed two controversial points here. The first is that press freedom should not be freedom for journalists alone, let alone for media proprietors, full-time administrators, public and rulers, to determine what shall be said and how. The public as a body cannot be portrayed as a threat to press freedom, simply because they have as much right to a determining role in communications as have journalists themselves.

Whether or not this is accepted will depend, academically at least, on the conception of journalistic underpinning attitudes towards the public (including the attitude of the public towards themselves. In particular, it will depend on the importance attached to the role of press freedom in the concept of nation building. If communication is seen primarily as the transmission of a body of fixed and certain knowledge by informed communicators and rulers to uninformed publics, then the idea that the public should be free to determine what shall be communicated will be seen as an inappropriate, anaemic and damaging ambition. How can the "ignorant" make rational decisions?

But if communication is less concerned with the transmission of a set or body of facts - and of course this varies from topic to topic - than with the development of the thought, feelings and ability of individual members of the public, then it is clear that a much less hierarchical approach to communicating messages is needed. The view that communications is not, beyond a certain basic level, about the ordinary transmission of information so much as getting people to think and find out for themselves, and so educate themselves, is quite compatible with the repressive or at best condescending atmosphere which reigns in most media establishments, and which deprives the public of any incentive to defend their own ideas and speak their minds. That people should be encouraged, not just permitted, to think for themselves is another of those clichés to which nearly everyone in the media is prepared to subscribe in principle, but a substantial and extensive freedom is the one indispensable condition of this principle being turned into a reality. This freedom must be above all freedom for those who are supposed to be the principal beneficiaries from the communication of ideas – the public themselves.

Hence, press freedom, and therefore journalistic power, must be a cake in which the people have a major share. If we are serious in wanting to encourage people to think for themselves as a first step towards development, we cannot possibly accept a situation in which the people are from the start being told what they ought to think about for themselves and very often how they ought to think about it as well. The implications of this approach are in fact very radical. The reason is that press freedom as it is understood here involves a respect for the formal principles of freedom of opinion and openness of debate to enable all the social classes in Africa to become the spectators of their own behaviour.

The second controversial element in the conception of press freedom being put forward is that it does not seek to eliminate personal bias from communications. It does not demand from either journalists or the public that they conform to unattainable and "undesirable" standards of neutrality or detachment. A distinction needs to be made here between neutrality and objectivity. Objectivity, in the sense of a respect for facts, and a certain standard of honesty in the treatment of evidence, is an obviously desirable quality for communication to cultivate. But neutrality or impartiality, in the sense of a demand that journalists and the public do not take sides and do not allow interpretation or opinion (or bias, or prejudice) to contaminate the pure stream of facts is an absurdity. The role of theory, or hypothesis, and interpretation is now generally accepted to be an irreducible element in even the most dispassionate and factual sciences. Heroic, quixotic efforts made to convert several humane studies into quantifying sciences have invariably failed and are doomed to fail. This is because these studies have been based on the quite mistaken belief that value judgements could be eliminated from these studies.

It is time that illusion was abandoned because it is a weapon against dissidence and unorthodoxy in journalism. Journalists who have made no secret of their political or religious commitments have frequently been hounded on the grounds that they have shown "bias" or "partiality", especially if the bias has been so-called "anti-establishmentarian." Everyone displays bias of one kind or another, and if some type of bias goes "undetected", that is only because it harmonizes so neatly with the "common sense" or conventional wisdom of the age. But as anyone with any knowledge whatsoever of the history of sociology of ideas will recognize, there is no reason to assume that the dominant orthodoxy of an age is more illuminating or closer to the truth than less familiar, and therefore more conspicuous, opinions. Of course, it is true that those with unorthodox and in particular, with radical, political views are most likely to be the objects of the conformist campaigns against bias; this form of conservative intolerance is certainly not unknown in other fields.

What press freedom requires is not the suppression of personal bias or commitment, which produces only dullness and patently fake neutrality, but the tolerance of a whole variety of different biases, commitments and approaches to ensure press freedom grows in depth and not in shreds and patches.

Chapter 2

Why Does Freedom Of The Press Matter?

From what has already been said, it ought to be clear why press freedom matters from the point of view of human communication itself. An atmosphere of flexibility, of openness, of readiness to experiment, to listen to and engage with unorthodox and dissident opinions - this is the essence of a healthy political community. There are so many powerful pressures for unquestioning conformity outside journalism that it is essential that people should find within it at least a margin of freedom within which they can develop their own potential for self-direction and independence - independence of thought, action and personality.

This battery of openness is also the precondition of development itself. From the suspicion with *which* so many authorities in "political party" hierarchies and military oligarchies look on journalism, and the limpet - like tenacity with which most rulers cling to the weedy rocks of the conservative self-celebrating formulae, to the arid routines of long, emotion-tapping speeches and above all to their own power, one might suppose that Moses had brought these methods down from the mountain along with the Ten Commandments. One might be forgiven for imagining that the orthodoxies of journalism possess the same certainty as the deductions of arithmetic or geometry. What is striking is that the whole area of communication, both what should be said and how, is an area of uncertainty and controversy. At the theoretical level, fundamental questions are being asked and debated with a real sense of urgency and excitement. Yet this hardly affects the attitudes of most rulers in Africa.

Experiment and free speech usually arouse hostility and are often suppressed brutally. Yet it is only through active experiment and a free flow of ideas which can give body and weight to a theoretical argument or position, that we can see clearly what journalism as a tool of modernization ought to be and what forms both ought to take.

Openness is likewise indispensable if the mass media are to perform their most important social function. Whatever specific function particular arms of the media may have, there is one general obligation which falls upon them all. It is their business to be critical. For them to do no more than pass on speeches, music and bodies of "knowledge" as if these constituted some kind of sacred and unquestionable gospel, is a fundamental betrayal of their primary duty to Africa. It becomes particularly aching and dehumanizing when this debased communication is charged with the typical propaganda reaching epidemic proportions.

It is no doubt a paradox that it is just this quality of danger, challenge and even outrage which sums up journalism's most important potential contribution to society. Criticism and challenge are always apt to be resented. The powerful and the established seldom take kindly to any criticism and can be expected to try either to suppress or at least discredit it. Even America's powerful Richard Nixon never did otherwise. The proper response to such attacks, when directed against journalists, is not only the apologetic or the defensive. The function has not fallen into disuse. Journalism serves society well, not through subservience, not through propping up its dogmas, but by subjecting them to hard questioning and debate. But this is no reason for supposing that its essential critical function is useless, destructive, or subversive.

If, however, we are looking for the reason why most people outside journalism in Africa are supremely indifferent to questions of press freedom and openness within it, this is either because they do not share this salient view of the social function and relevance of journalism or they are simply dozing on their easy arm-chairs after a great meal belching intermittently to prove that they were not quite asleep.

Only if a quite different view of the social purposes of communication is taken can the importance of press freedom be understood. On this view, the social function of the instruments of social communication is critical, questioning, experimental and innovatory. It is at the same time geared primarily to the needs of society as complete human beings, as individuals and as citizens. And if these are, or ought to be, the principal commitments of journalism, then clearly both the freedom of journalists and public, and the autonomy of the press system as a whole are of great importance – not only to journalists, but to society as a whole. It thus becomes totally unrealistic to imagine that the realisation of these aims is compatible with either a high degree of control by government or the state, or with a high degree of dependence upon private sponsorship. Unfortunately, at present both the control and the dependence are increasing' and both are inspired, or reinforced, by the wrong belief that the chief social function of the press is to serve the immediate or future needs of the-powers-that-be. In any wider view of society within Africa and beyond its needs, it is clear that there is cause for alarm at the rate press freedom is diminishing. These tendencies must be opposed, not in the name of the total social irresponsibility of journalism, but because the independence and freedom of the press is the necessary condition of performing its essential critical and human tasks in what is hotly sold as "African Democracy".

However, limited that independence and freedom may be in practice, anyone who values the human commitments of journalism ought to fight hard against any tendency which threatens to reduce it still further.

The official version of "free" African society and history is, of course, very different from this. According to this account such lofty principles as freedom, tolerance and democracy have nothing in common with anything so sordid as economic development in African states, or even with political turbulence and disorder. If African states today enjoy any freedom and tolerance whatsoever than others less fortunate emergent nations, say in the runaway Middle East or Latin America, that is because they inherited some liberal traditions from their turbulent past which they cannot toss aside lightly. That is to say, some Western institutions which "imprison" leaders to be tolerant of a measure of free speech were inherited from the colonial past and the populace is so used to these institutions that the inheritance regimes, no matter how sanguinary, find it troubling to toss them aside lightly.

Some of the more politically "sophisticated" myth-mongers like to counter-balance alarming economic stagnation and political repression with reassurance. The traditional blood-chilling phrases such as to "destroy society" or anti-social layabouts whose chief aim is to incite destruction of "all-that-is-best-in-our-society" are generally the empty words used to intimidate and edge out objective journalists. And the minorities of daring nationalistic journalists have been allowed to run amok. And firm action from any ruler will quickly stamp this out. This horror-comic account of journalistic life in Africa would be more amusing if it were not so widely mistaken for "subversion" by the powers-that-be, the bootlickers and the ignorant masses. To say that many African intellectual men-of-power have joined in this public chorus of anti-media feelings would be to do them less than justice.

Reactionary intellectual opportunists have not merely followed this trend; they have been among its rued leaders and inspirers, and few sights or sounds in contemporary Africa have been more nauseous than the spectacle of intellectuals adding their individual cadenzas of hostility to this chorus of abuse. Ii is nauseous because one might expect more in the way of fairness and understanding from those who, after all, have a direct responsibility to, as well as for, journalists, and who do not have the public's or the politician's excuse of having few opportunities for direct contact with them. But this has become one of the most shameful contradictions in journalism, that so many intellectual hooligans apparently dislike and despise those who promote the sharing of ideas. Intellectuals baying for journalists' blood do not make a pretty sight.

Discontents and their repression

The most extensive and significant kind of discontent has been the disconcertingly slow pace at which social welfare is being tackled. And, in fact and in right, African journalists are expected to raise loud cries against the prestigious hypocrisy called national unity, peace and stability; organs of indoctrination called institutions of learning, trade unions and press; manipulative hierarchies called private enterprises; conformity called status; lives of repressively quiet desperation called progress and success.

Case after case of injustice has been documented by the International Press Institute (IPI): the use of torture as a means of interrogation has officially been admitted and sanctioned, and hundreds of journalists have suffered from

15

the brutality of the Army and the Police in Azania (South Africa), Zimbabwe, Central African Empire, etc.

That this is not fanciful alarmism can be deduced from the fact that at least every African country has records of mutinous journalistic dissent.

Dissent, both political and (in the narrow sense) non-political, has been increasingly the object of police harassment and legal attack.

At best it has become routine for some of the demonstrators to be charged with such trivial but conveniently open-ended offences as obstruction, subversion, or conduct liable to cause a breach of the peace. Such fake charges are a generalized propaganda barrage against permissiveness in most African societies.

In several African countries there have been innumerable complaints of police brutality in the handling of journalists in the past few years. In Sierra Leone, they are simply killed.

Attacks on Press Freedom

Compared to various indications of a growing toughness and disregard for citizens' rights and freedom on the part of African states, what has been happening in the world of African journalism, may not appear to be very important, but it would be foolish to underestimate its significance. The journalistic sphere is one that is both particularly vulnerable, yet in which the principle of freedom is traditionally accepted as relevant and appropriate. It ought therefore to be possible to mount an effective defence of freedom within communications. But if freedom can be successfully attacked in journalism, that can only presage even more effective assaults elsewhere. And press freedom has been under attack in recent years.

First, there has been the attack on journalists, which has not been a merely verbal one, but has involved a determined attempt, led by politicians, "intellectuals" and bureaucrats, to eliminate press discontent by direct repression. It is naive to suppose that repression necessarily does not work – at least in the short run whenever there is a strong-arm response to journalists' discontent.

Second, there have been incessantly brutal attacks on press publications. At times all publications of a newspaper are seized and the stencils all burnt by the police or "gendarmes". Familiar measures of repression like these make the media to lose their boldness since verbiage can hold no successful argument with the gun or with a typical Nazi-style torture cell. And, the only way to survive under such cruel circumstances, some African journalists think, is to practise cosmetic journalism, in so far as it remains at the level of sensation, is superficial, trying to attract attention by eroticism and violence, lacking an inner life, answering the cheap demands of publicity, appeals to people's instincts and thus making itself a mere consumer product.

Unless we believe that freedom is a fringe benefit which ought to be sacrificed to the requirements of "order", and that democracy means nothing more substantial than the right to vote once in five years (and in practice many people do believe this)we shall recognize that both freedom and democracy must exist in the journalism sphere as in every other part of society, and we shall not view with complacency or indifference those forecasts at present which so strongly threaten their existence and their future. This would mean that instead of standing emaciated, inert and largely speechless like the victim of a stroke, the African mass media must bray at the sinners who make believe that Africa is just marsh land on which it is impossible to build.

The independence and openness of the media, and therefore their vital critical and human purposes, are threatened both from outside the media sphere, and more ominously and quite as seriously, from within it. There is an apparent paradox here, but we are concerned with the freedom of individuals as well as the independence of institutions, and the autonomy of an institution is, of course, quite compatible with repression and intolerance within it. What is more, even those who have the prime responsibility for maintaining the freedom and independence of the press have largely defaulted on that responsibility and have been collaborating with outside forces to achieve the distortion of media channels and their publications in the interest of private economic, political and military needs of individuals and the state.

Five or six possible sources of danger to freedom can be identified in Africa, three external and three internal. From outside, the media have to cope with the claw-hold pressure exerted upon it by the state and government, by something rather vaguely called "public opinion", and by the owners and controllers of business and industry. From within, freedom can be menaced by those who have the power and authority in journalism or by the staff more generally, or by the public. All these are possible if not actual threats, and we will consider them in turn to see exactly where the real dangers lie.

These groups, or pressures, do overlap quite extensively with each other. This is particularly so in case of the external forces. The states, public opinion and business/industry interact with each other in such a way that in many specific situations it is hard to separate one from another. The government and other authorities are inevitably responsive to some extent to vocal public opinion, or to what they imagine public opinion to be. Thus external pressures are, most of the time, mediated through the media's internal structures of power, and this conjunction of external pressures (often financial) with internal press authority presents a formidably entrenched and fortified alliance which it is not easy to oppose effectively.

The State and the Press

In every discussion the state is often equated with the government, and vice versa. But this is to underestimate the resources and ramifications of the elaborate and subtle machinery by which our African societies are shaped and steered and controlled without very obviously appearing to be so. The forms of "freedom" and the fictions of "democracy" are "carefully" preserved and constantly praised, often with perfectly ignorant sincerity, but they function as a facade behind which the less palatable realities of heavy-handed power can lie decorously concealed .So, ,there is the well-known distinction between the "dignified" and "efficient" parts of the political system which is too neat , in that it is so often through the dignified , and extensibly independent institutions of the state that aims of government and industry are most securely achieved , just because such institutions command respect which could never be won bodies under the direct and open control of the government of the day

These bodies should enjoy a genuine degree of independence to show that African states, in normal circumstances are not too heavily governed. Of course, the restrictions on their independence, when times are normal, need only to be tacitly acknowledged on both sides. In times of strain and crisis, however, these bodies can run up against the limits of official tolerance. The usually loose reins can be tightened, and any traditional "gentlemanly" compacts could be temporally replaced by the grimmer methods of censorship and political *diktat*. The most important of all these semi-independent institutions should be the superfluous government-owned and controlled radios and newspapers whose history is at times studded with crises in which the requirements of governments come into conflict with the media institutions' "professional commitments" to honest reporting and free discussion. In cases of conflict, pimps within the press sell its freedom cheaply in the corridors of power.

Freedom has now become an old- fashioned luxury which a country undergoing rapid development can no longer afford, they say. And this saying makes the press cower, tremble and develop cold feet.

Is the state neutral?

The influence and control of the state over mediated communications had increased, is increasing, and ought to be (though seldom is) staunchly resisted. That is the burden of this chapter. It now remains to say more explicitly why such resistance is desirable.

In general some media bureaucrats, who have been as active as anyone in reducing the autonomy of the press have been frank enough to admit , in however bland and reassuring a manner , that this is what is happening . But to them it seems a desirable or at worst a "necessary" trend. A measure of freedom must be given up in order to make the mass media more "relevant" and responsive to the "national interest". Or, more subtly, they argue that unless the media adapt themselves in these ways they would lose even that limited measure of freedom which they now possess. It is, in others words, a policy of appeasement which they recommend in the belief that they are rescuing at least half of the loaf of freedom.

What such an argument assumes, rather than asserts, is that the demands of the state or government actually are the demands of the "nation," because the state represents the nation at that given historic moment; and in the other equation, that the needs of national development can then be identified with the needs of the nation. By "nationally determined," they mean in fact, worked out by the government of the day with the stereotyped civil servants of the departments of Information, and with an essentially executive and subordinate roles being played by conservative journalists.

We can see just no reason or excuse to accept either that the state is representative of the nation, or that the requirements of "economic development" can be identified with the national needs. Chaotic African politics witnessed in Rwanda's genocidal wars, Liberia and Sierra Leone's fratricidal civil wars are not a novel phenomenon. The whole liberal theory of the state which underpins the respect it receives from docile establishment bodies seems false and empty when viewed in the African continent.

Chapter 3

Patterns of Repression

A renewal of faith in common human nature, in its
potentialities in general, and in its power and truth, is a surer
bulwark against totalitarianism than a demonstration of
material success or a devious worship of special legal and
political forms.
(John Dewey)

So far, the pattern outlined is that of the shrinking
independence of the media. An autonomy which, even during
the colonial days, was always limited, and flourished most
healthily during the years of African nationalism, has been
steadily reduced by the multiple pressures of the state and
industry, and most significantly, by industry through the
agency of the African state whose role is to make the society
safe for capitalist exploitation. The critical, sceptical,
enquiring aspects of journalism have been neglected, and the
principle that journalism should be responsive to the needs
and demands of those who actually experience it - the public-
has been ignored (all in the favour of efforts to "produce
citizens the nation needs"). This is political suicide to flush
the free press out of life because it is a major component of
any worthy human society.

These developments have met with extraordinarily little
resistance. As we have seen the media establishments, the
public intellectuals and judiciary which might have been
expected to lead such resistances, have for the most part
cooperated willingly or acquiesced and at times even eagerly

adapted communications to these cramping requirements. The story is not one of external aggression and internal resistance, so much as of thinly veiled threats and aggressive designs which do not need to be carried out because collaboration within the besieged citadel makes them unnecessary. Opportunists and journalists alike have vied with others to gain funds, posts of responsibility and contracts from the government and industry and have delighted to boast of their efforts to provide "nationalistic" brands of journalism even when they do not more than echo the views and opinions of the authorities that be.

Let us now consider the other side of that record-the behaviour of press corps within their own press institutions. For if, as was argued earlier, press freedom is something in which the public and journalists ought to have the major share, it is clear that the behaviour of the press-man and woman in the use of media power is of crucial importance. Do they use their power and authority to protect and extend press freedom? Or do they opportunistically use it to punish dissenting views and obstruct the spread of democratic forms and methods in their media establishments? There is no doubt in my mind as to the answer which a growing body of evidence suggests: the most direct attacks on press freedom have come from the media authorities themselves, and it is their gross and arbitrary power which continues to constitute the most serious threat to press freedom. It is no doubt a bitter and outrageous irony that those who ought to be the spokesmen and defenders of press freedom in Africa should play this miserable role.

Who are these "authorities"? Structures differ a bit, but obviously editors and press owners must be included, particularly where these are influential posts. Broadly speaking, they govern the media. Thus, it is often true, in a

24

sense, to say that these institutions are self-governing, but self-government, however, is not media democracy. Self-government in this context usually means oligarchy or even autocracy, in many media houses.

Victimisation

But concessions to the pressure for reform of press laws, or even self-examination, are exceptional. Most African authorities have relied on simple repression as their principal weapon in restoring "normality" and in preventing future agitation by the press. It is clear that everybody who has a right to control the press has acquired what one may call the police mentality. That is to say, they have usually adopted the deterrent method of "preventing trouble". Be tough this time", the repressive argument goes, and there may never be a next time". With this view in mind, the authorities unleash an orgy of victimisation. It is happening in South Africa; it was the case in Amin's Uganda; we saw it in Marcias Nguema's Equatorial Guinea; we continue to experience it in many other African countries.

So the victimisation of a few individual journalists has normally been the chosen method of punishing and weaning the mass media. The word victimisation is appropriate because those selected for punishment have often all too evidently been chosen on an arbitrary and ill-informed basis. The fairness of punishing any handful of individuals as a reprisal for mass action is open to question. But what is manifestly an abuse of justice is when the handful include individuals who could not even conceivably be described as "ring leaders". That the arrests, detentions without trial, brutal beatings or dismissals and incarcerations constitute an offence against the principles of natural justices is beyond question. Since it also involves the temporary or permanent exclusion of some journalists from the press establishments, it also offends against the principles of press freedom.

Victimization is unjust. It does not follow that it is ineffective. On the contrary, this arbitrary selective punishment of a few journalists may have had the intended effect of deterring many others from following their "bad" example. The quieter and submissive condition of so many arms of the media in the post-independent years or so may owe something to the success of the policy of repression. And if this is what the African authorities themselves believe, then it is certain that we have not heard the last of it. It will be the normal method of responding to press dissent. At the time the repression provokes protest and outrage, and in some cases, this protest may muster enough strength actually to bring the arbitrary victimization to an end. But this is unusual. For the most part, the authorities' tenacity in pursuing their victims has not been matched by the equivalent staying power of the press. The continuously changing composition of the press corps alone makes this difficult.

There is a further aspect of this policy which requires comment, and that is the forms through which it is operated. Typically, these forms are pseudo-legal. They appear to imitate the forms of the law itself, and by doing so they acquire an air of legitimacy and impartiality. But whatever may be true of the law itself, it must be said that in the case of these press mock-ups the appearance of neutrality and impartiality is completely bogus. Those who, as it were, make the charges and bring the prosecutions also appoint those who act as judge and jury. These bodies are neither independent, nor do they even observe the normal rights and procedures which prevail in the law itself. As it is often the case, the disciplinary and appeals procedures for journalists are similarly weighted against them and in favour of the rulers who are in themselves law, party, political principle and all else.

Bias in appointment-making

The cases about which least is known are those in which a radical journalist is not appointed at all on account of his views. Like most important decision-making processes in the Ministries of Information, the business of making appointments is shrouded in careful secrecy, lobbying and back-stabbing. Much informal discussion and telephoning precedes the formal meetings and drawing up of the appointment lists, and the outcome of the process may well be determined by the informal rather than the formal consultation.

It is not unreasonable to think that political and other non-professional considerations have entered into these appointment cases, even when there is the absence of decisive evidence to this effect. Few beams of light have reached these dark places where political dimensions to appointments predominate to the extent that one can guess the degree to which political factors have entered into the making of these appointments. This is a flagrant contravention of the principle that appointments in the mass media should be made on professional grounds, without reference to the politics or creed of the appointees.

It is no doubt agreeable when corrupt, and inefficient people are appointed to big jobs and are found to be loyal persons with whom everyone in political authority can "collaborate". Equally, all of us would like at times to be in the position where we could veto the appointment of someone with whom we "would not wish to work." Yet it is an undeniable fact that such universal harmony is rare even with a single work in life, and that when such a criterion is taken seriously many of the most able and brilliant journalists suffer. Such criterion is not a journalistic one. It is simply a euphemistic method of excluding the awkward customer, whether the awkwardness be political or personal or both. This is why in the end it is easy for the authorities to adjudge any act of criticism, any challenge to their authority, as "rebellion" or a threat to "peace and order"- a very elastic way of using words.

This raises, above all, the question of: with what "constitution" do the authorities get their right to expect that everyone shall always operate within the constitutional boundaries which they themselves have decreed. Words like "constitutional" contrive to give the impression that media instituti0ns are democracies, governed with the consent of the governed. This is, of course, not so. The "constitutional arrangements which prevail in media establishments are not democratic, nor were they arrived at democratically. They are the product of the oligarchies who rule, and expect everyone else to conform to the rules which they have made, and which constitute "constitutional" authority in their hands. The mere fact that some people have a paper entitlement to make decisions and the rules does not make their rule less arbitrary or more democratic; nor does it entitle them to label as "disruption" any action taken outside the rules which they have made and enforce upon others.

Meanwhile, it must be said that the "constitutional" implication that there can be freedom of speech but not necessarily freedom of action by the free press clearly reduces free speech to an ineffectual charade. For what can possibly be the purpose or valve of freedom of speech which is not also accompanied by freedom of action?

Freedom which allows someone to hold and even to express an opinion, but not to act upon it, is all too obviously a safety-valve which allows the team of discontent to escape uselessly into the empty air. It is the freedom to grumble - impotently -and a great deal less than we have the right to expect from those who are supposed to have a very special and professional commitment to a real and substantial freedom of opinion.

Freedom of criticism

Several cases of shabby treatment meted out to journalists show that even the limited freedom which allows criticism and opposition provided it is unrelated to action is not necessarily expressed. It is clear that authorities who have in most cases, when according to their legal linguistics, been affronted by "subversive" journalists, did take the steps along what could very easily prove to be a word of ever-widening repression and intolerance.

Many episodes in various African countries indicate how bitterly the authorities resent criticism of their own behaviour and how bitterly they will grasp at the opportunity to punish or expel their critics, however numerous they may be and however modest their criticisms. It is beside the point whether the criticisms are justified. That is a matter on which no doubt more than one view is possible. What is startling, and revealing, is the sheer vindictiveness of the response to criticism.

Most journalists very soon learn to keep quiet, know that there is a risk attached to "embarrassing" rulers, and even more, substantial risk in offending one's political boss on whom one's future appointment and promotion prospects so largely depend.

Press Freedom and the Power Structure

In times of crisis, journalists are often too surprised to discover how far their freedom is dependent upon the benevolence of their political bosses, private employers, the police and the justice department. "Easy constraints" turn harsh and the collective power of the media staff turns out to be purely ambiguously advisory.

Decision on cases against journalists are often inspired by political considerations or a purely personal animus; and this high- handed attitude demonstrates how easily an arbitrary and unfair decision can be taken with walls of secrecy shielding the quasi-judicial decision-taking processes and persons from either inspection or criticism.

In such cases the "just" decision-makers do not respect the human rights principle of free speech, and they do not observe the reasonable requirement that justice shall not only be done but also be seen to be done. They prefer to shroud their decisions and their processes in a fog of secrecy and non-communication.

In some African states Information Ministers may have control over appointments, promotions and dismissals which is near-absolute. And professional journalists may understand that it is not uncommon for them to be even consulted at all about these happenings. Even when consulted find themselves simply overruled. As a result, the usual appointment procedures are so politically tinged that they become too far from being impartial and fair.

These natural and normal attitudes of politicians, bureaucrats and administrators, private employers and conservative media heads are fundamentally at odds with the climate that journalism requires a climate of openness and unfettered argument and controversy. Such a climate can only flourish when power in communication is in the hands of those whose first commitment is to communication, not merely to the needs of the government and business or the bureaucratic ideals of order and efficiency. Power in communication ought to be in the hands of journalists and public, not professional, or even near-full-time administrators who see any new idea as "disruptive" or even a "trouble-maker".

Abuses of power, corruption, tribalism, nepotism, subversion, etc. cannot be prevented when the press which is supposed to bray out the sinners for prosecution is gagged.

Chapter 4

Whose Failures?

"A great nation cannot survive for long on a shifty and slippery foundation of self-deception and misinformation."
(William J. Lederer, Nation of Sheep, 1961)

At every level of existence, the manifestation of African manhood is retreating, making way for the prevalence for material things, for the harsh dynamics of abstractions constructed with the solid bricks of inconsistency and perversion. Media ethics in Africa are now faced with the designs of this culture that has twisted men's hearts, imbuing it with the insatiable desire for extreme freedom and irresponsibility towards this continent and towards mankind. The pursuit of unlimited pleasure breaks the traditional bounds of natural societies, embroiling human beings in a wild confusion of activity in which craziness takes on the daily flavour of the necessary norm-the desolation of a continent steeped in anguish and in violence.

The freedom of individual journalists and that of the press has come under sharp attack in our times, both directly from the public and press authorities and "indirectly" from the growing directive power of the state and the influence of "industry". How have the journalists themselves reacted to such attacks? This question has to be asked, for one cannot assume that the public and journalists will necessarily recognize that their freedom is currently in more than usual danger in this continent. Indeed, we should have to accept that the journalists as a group respond to these threats with all the alertness of an exceptionally complacent ostrich. The failure in giving the press its freedom comes from journalists, the public and the authorities.

Journalists' Unions

Wherever they have existed at all, the unions have shown themselves reluctant to investigate cases of "alleged" attacks on press freedom. When they have been persuaded to do so they have usually come up with an anodyne report, in which it turns out that nothing very bad has happened against journalists' freedom; anywhere there is one to be wrong, he the journalist or journalists.

Nor has the official position of the unions been any more reassuring than their day-to-day tactics of knowing if journalists are "moderate" and "responsible". At times journalists' unions have had little choice but to reaffirm the principle of press freedom in general terms, yet at the same time they have specifically refused to close the loopholes by which political and crypto-political criteria have been introduced into the making of media appointments. They have taken the view that other than purely journalistic considerations, including a man's ability to "get on" or cooperate with his colleagues, are relevant and ought to count in all appointments rather than elastic political rubrics which only help to erode press freedom.

A journalist has a right to communicate his subject as he wishes though he should avoid giving deliberate offence to those to whom he is communicating by allowing his objectivity to be swamped by, for example, his political or religious views. It would be naïve to imagine that in the event of a dispute it would be passionate "authorities" who would decide whether objectivity had been swamped. That, no doubt, would be a matter on which experts, the courts and press unions would claim the right to adjudicate. Allowing the-powers-that-be to adjudicate means an attempt to continue to subscribe to the threadbare myth that the media are communities of journalists within and out of which there can, by definition, be on serious conflicts of interests or interpretations of press freedom.

It would be unfair therefore, to take the performance and policies of the unions as an accurate reflection of opinion. Equally mistaken, however, is to rush to the opposite conclusion that the great body of journalists have rallied vigorously to the defence of their threatened colleagues when the need has arisen.

But a generalized resentment and sentiment in favour of change, expressed anonymously in response to a questionnaire, is a very different thing from running the risks inherent in opposing the oligarchies and administration of institutions at moments of tribal, national and international crises. This is commonplace when hysteria prevails and appeals for loyalty are blended with veiled threats as to the possible consequences of disloyalty. In these demanding circumstances it has almost invariably been the case that only a minority, and often a small minority of journalists and unions have been willing to incur these risks.

A further reason for this ineffectiveness, however, has been the failure of journalists and their unions to develop any collective methods of putting pressure on their "superiors and employers." The conventions of media professionalism and the myth of the press community prevent journalists from being itchy about adopting the tactics of the partial or complete withdrawal of labour by striking.

Relations with the Public

It remains a general truth, however, that the part played by the public in defending press freedom has been secondary to that played by individual journalists. It is secondary in importance, and it is most often secondary also in point of time. The public merely urges the press into the battle for press freedom while standing from a safe and distant place. Deprived of most fundamental freedom, a fear psychosis has overtaken the whole continent, be it under racist white minority or black rule. Not until after individual journalists have taken action to defend a colleague in "trouble" or being threatened, or to raise some major but neglected issue of press policy or freedom, do the public normally "involve" themselves. Even then, they do not involve themselves as a body or a majority in support of the journalist's course. It is only a minority which is likely to take such a stand. Many others, fearful of the rage which the journalist's publication may do, close ranks in support of the administration and the restoration of order and normality though they may logically and silently be in favour of the journalist's views. Thus in crises involving issues of press freedom and democracy, the journalists are the ones who play the crucial role, whether it be purely defensive or whether it involves raising some important yet dormant issue. The public is only stirred into secret sympathy after a journalist has been so mercilessly treated that it is impossible for all but the most incorrigible ostriches to ignore, And under such cruel circumstances public sympathies are muted or defeated either by the sheer obstinacy of the authorities, by their infinite capacity for diversion and delay, for shunting major issues into the sidings of endless deadlock within committees or within administrative processes.

Of course members of the public would indignantly deny this. It would be difficult, if not impossible, to find any of them who does not claim to have a strong belief in freedom of speech and opinion, in the exclusion of political criteria from the making of appointments, dismissals or judgements. However, the test must be not what general principle they nominally subscribe to, but how they respond when these and other principles of freedom of speech are under direct attack. From this type of test the majority of the public emerge with little credit. It has been left to a minority, often very small, to speak out in times of crisis; in fact, essentially they fail under pressure to uphold the principle of press freedom; some even sit cross-legged in the face of a harsh curtailment of their freedom.

Relations with Authorities

What of the methods (direct action and "constitutionalism") which have sometimes been employed? The use of force and disruption constitute the stock-in-trade of desperate official action against journalists viewed by authorities as being "unpatriotic". But if journalism is committed to anything, it is to reason and argument, and therefore cannot tolerate the introduction of force and coercion into its peaceful domain by authorities who claim to protect public freedom.

Journalism, as we have seen, is not blessed with any special immunity to the normal pressures of money and power, nor are its institutions models of government by open debate and argument.

It is a monstrous and hypocritical impertinence for authorities, from their positions of constitutionally sanctified power, to tell journalists that they must employ only reason.

For they do not, in their oligarchy, rule by virtue of their superior rationality. They do indeed hold the constitutional authority, but that bland, reassuring word "constitutional" should not mislead us, By what right are journalists expected to conform to a militarily decreed "constitution" for which their consent has never been sought or given, and which, in any case, explicitly deprives them of all real power? General Buhari's media gagging Decree No.4 in Nigeria in the 80s does not need any explanation.

The argument from constitutionals is really nothing more than at best, a piece of mystification, and at worst, an unusually cynical fraud. What is the relationship of Paul Biya and respect for his 1996 "Constitution"? He either disrespects or modifies it at will to ordain himself as "President for Life." This is simply to say that politicians and military rulers have come to expect too great a degree of docility from the public, as if it was the job of journalists to do no more than sit and listen and ask the occasional polite question: what are your impressions about...?. The constant blanket denunciations of "violence" by rulers are hypocritical, since they are not pacifists and have never objected when epidemic violence has been used against journalists by their political militia called "national armies."

Let me conclude, therefore, that none of the arguments usually put forward for regarding journalists as a threat, or even "the threat", to press freedom carries much weight. Behind all the agitated babbling about "mob rule" lies the fear and hostility of those who see in journalists' demands for press democracy a threat, not to freedom, but to their own established power and privileges.

If there is one conclusion towards which the argument of this essay leads irresistibly it is that there can be no safeguarding or extending of freedom in the mass media until its institutions have become democratized. Press freedom without press democracy is insecure and inadequate, no matter the intellectual hubbub.

Democracy implies not only the devolution of power through widespread participation. It also implies openness. Procedures of decision-taking, instead of being concealed behind closed doors, should be as open as possible, so that all those affected shall at least know what is being done and thus have the opportunity to express their views on the subject. Openness too is a basic ideal of communication.

Chapter 5

Conclusion: Press Censorship and Social Equilibrium

"...effective feedback may be crucial to political stability...
where feedback in a political system has either broken down or
been blocked, serious consequences have arisen for the system
as a whole."
(Graham Mytton, Mass Communication in Africa, 1983)

Press censorship which is a strand of press control has
contributed in no small way to reduce newsmen to a false
status of irrational, unpatriotic and irresponsible individuals.
No other solid reason accounts for this than the uncouth and
unprofessional mutilation of information written by
journalists and censored by authorities who have no training,
knack or insight into what constitute news in the first place.

A small mews item- or perhaps a serious one which
cracks in a province - has to go through a reporter who writes
it. It is then passed through the Senior Divisional Officer for
perusal and approval. From then it goes to the Provincial
Delegate of Information for the same scrutiny and possible
visa. It goes through the same process of censorship and
gatekeeping when it arrives in the radio station.

What this inevitably amounts to is that by the time the
news item or story gets to the Radio station, it has lost both
its intrinsic news valve and the element of timeliness. And
who doubts why the censorship by authorities whose
knowledge of press functions is at best hazy and at worst
smattering? Such men, empowered by existing paper

41

instructions, seek to blot out or truncate a news story whose moral value is depraving, that could threaten public order and breach the peace of the land. These are the moral and ethical grounds on which they think they are qualified to censor information written by pressmen to be consumed by reasonable people.

The common misadventure however, is that most of the authorities who claim to tamper or censor information do so in the supreme interest of securing their positions, than the latent will of guaranteeing the peace and public morals. For, one could ask a series of chilling questions: Is the authority more patriotic and peace-loving than the journalist? How many people have gone berserk or on a rampage in the streets because they read a story the authorities did not want published? Or what right has an authority to claim a better mastery of the social responsibility of the press than the pressman who earns a livelihood out of his news vocation?

Despite the parochialism and the sentimentalism displayed by censors, some people think that press censorship still has its raison d'être. There are no polemics when one considers the good intentions of such a delicate and intricate exercise.

But the increasing number of blank pages of many newspapers whose information is spooned off by censorship executives, disquiets those who hunger and thirst for the naked truth and muzzles those who unveil serious palpable information for societal good.

There can be no salutary claim of press pluralism when the content- which is the bedrock of diversity in appreciation- smacks of monolithic ideas because of sullen censorship. Press censorship which goes beyond gate-keeping against defamation and issues of national security find no place in a society where freedom should reign, where law rules and where the public is considered as rational and not zombie-like. John Milton's ideal should be upheld: "Truth and falsehood should grapple in the market place of ideas" and the public would distinguish blatant lies from sacred truths. In this way, even highly placed journalists involved in tight censorship will now learn to be procurers of news, not censors of news.

Press Censorship and Social Equilibrium

We do not need to be reminded that without balance, we cannot maintain an erect posture. This posture is maintained as a result of co-ordinating a clear-flowing stream of information about the position and activity of the human body. This line of reasoning finds full expression in the domain of the press and its contribution to social equilibrium. There is a guarantee from the proceeding analogy that it is only when the information channels are faithfully and compassionately free-flowing that the human emotions become steady, deep, perpetual and vivifying to the soul as the natural pulse is to the body. A healthy and active society would jealously guard its state if only it indiscriminately received any information from anywhere, at any time, no matter its kind.

The sense of balance or equilibrium of any complete human body is wholly dependent upon the multiple sensations from its sense organs like the skin, nose, muscles, eyes or from a portion of the inner ear, called the semi-circular canals. Similarly, the sense of equilibrium of any human society is hinged on the scrupulous accuracy its information organs maintain.

The most vital contributions to the body's equilibrium are from the inner ear as those of any worthy human society are its eyes and ears - the communication media. Hence, these organs cannot rightly be looked upon as thorns to the stability of the body or society when they are functioning naturally, and are properly organised like the human ear. It has three semi-circular canals, which are curbed tubes set at right angles in a plane. These canals have dilated ends furnished with sensitive nerve receptors and hair- tipped cells to arrest any information that comes their way. The information organs in the living society must be similarly and alertly supplied with "fluid" which moves with each movement of the head. Therefore, to report fully and accurately about society and its activities, the information organs must move with that society.

When the head rotates, displaced fluid presses more on some hairy cells than others. And it is known from experience the position our head has assumed - downwards, erect, sideways. But if we whirl around rapidly, the splashing of the fluid which continues in our ears after we stop, leaves us confused and dizzy. We must at this time wait until the fluid calms down before we know where we are in relation to information bearing the confused and dizzy state of the body whose information ran throughout the ear without being registered, analysed in depth, interpreted and responded to objectively.

If the ear, by mistake, plunged into an avalanche of sensationalism and inflated the information to intolerable limits, the critical capacities of the brain will be made numb. The individual will become mad. Also, if the information about the position of the body were left porous and pitted, leached of its substance like laterite in the dry season and repeated by the ear with a tiresome frequency with the hope that this is the only way of making the head approve it, the information will ring so much in the mind that nothing more will be heard. The leached information will block the entry of any other information. Thus, information is the fuel that does keep the wheel of any civilisation turning.

Nobody, no matter how highly placed in society, by dint of whatever virtues, should over-assume that he has the breadth of knowledge and background to understand and direct everything - information inclusive. It is an ungainly attempt to use or pressure the information media to use scandal-mongering, scurrilous libel and outright falsehood in the name of social stability. The information organs must look at news through glasses that are neither rose-coloured nor smoked, but in the white light of impartial and scrupulously honest observation.

The information media must not only tell society that it is erect, but that it is falling whenever it is actually falling .They must not root the cause and- effect orientation of information in intentionally bulky errors to permit readers or the audience to lick their lips over human misery by telling white lies. In fact, the press would be soliciting costs which must be paid for in the coin of other priceless values if it (the press) heedlessly attempts to short- circuit genuine explanations beyond the metes and bounds of fixed truths. Nor should the media pursue its greedy interests by playing the role of the conformists. Societies, it is said, are not built or improved by conformists.

The information media direct the thoughts, feelings, and aspirations of a great part of mankind. For this very reason, the distortions of truth by organs of information can have incalculable consequences -leading mankind up to ruin (in our present state of suffering, sorrow on sorrow), never to glory. It should be cause for disquiet if the media failed to be a potent weapon against human injustices or one of the cornerstones of democracy in Africa where political pluralism has been mistakenly or mischievously interpreted to mean organizing a coterie of friends to form inconsequential political parties so as to please the West.

Appendix

My Final Statement of Shared Purpose

After extended examination by African journalists themselves of the character of journalism at the end of the twentieth century, I offer this common understanding of what defines the profession. I may sound repetitive here. But, I deem it essential to home these shared professional concerns more forcefully since every African politician nowadays sings the hum-drum of democracy.

The central purpose of journalism is to provide citizens with accurate and reliable information they need to function in a free society.

This encompasses myriad roles - helping define community, creating common language and common knowledge, identifying a community's goals, heroes and villains, and pushing people beyond complacency. This purpose also involves other requirements, such as being entertaining, serving as watchdog and offering voice to the voiceless.

Over time, African journalists have developed nine core principles to meet the task of functioning usefully in a competitive electronic age. They comprise what we might describe as the theory of journalism in this age of media globalization:

1) The First Obligation of any journalist is to the Truth

Democracy depends on citizens having reliable, accurate facts put in a meaningful context. Journalism does not pursue truth in an absolute or philosophical sense, but it can - and must - pursue it in a practical sense. This "journalistic truth" is a process that begins with the professional discipline of assembling and verifying facts. Then journalists try to convey a fair and reliable account of their meaning, valid for now, subject to further investigation. Journalists should be as transparent as possible about sources and methods so that audiences can make their own assessment of the information. Even in a world of expanding voices, accuracy is the foundation upon which everything else is built - context, interpretation, comment, criticism, analysis and debate. The truth, over time, emerges from this forum. As citizens encounter an ever greater flow of data, they have more need - not less - for identifiable sources dedicated to verifying that information and putting it in context. In Africa today, politicians learn to be professional liars. And this tendency to fool the public compels journalists to pursue the truth with Koranic fidelity.

2) Serve Citizens and the Public Interest First

As a matter of generality, citizenship in Africa poses problems of definition. Are you a citizen of country A only when your "tribesman" is President or for ever? Are you a citizen of country B because you speak the language spoken by some of its inhabitants, and can thus be trucked into that country to vote for a candidate seeking elective office.

While news organizations answer to many constituencies, including politicians, advertisers and shareholders, the journalists in those organizations must maintain allegiance to citizens and the larger public interest above any other if they are to provide the news without fear or favour. This commitment to citizens first is the basis of news organization's credibility, the implied covenant that tells the audience the coverage is not slanted for friends or advertisers.

Commitment to citizens also means journalism should present a representative picture of all constituent groups in society. Ignoring certain citizens has the effect of disenfranchising them. The theory underlying the modern news industry has been the belief that credibility builds a broad and loyal audience, and that economic success follows in turn. In that regard, the business people in a news organization also must nurture - not exploit - their allegiance to the audience ahead of other considerations.

3) Monitor the powerful and Offer Voice to the voiceless

Journalism has an overwhelming capacity to serve as watchdog over those whose power and position most affect citizens. The Founders recognized this to be a rampart weapon against despotism when they ensured an independent press; courts have affirmed it in countries like Nigeria; citizens rely on it as it is the case in Senegal. As journalists, we have an obligation to protect this watchdog freedom by not demeaning it in frivolous use or exploiting it for "food" or commercial gain.

4) Provide Society with a Forum for Comment, Criticism and Compromise

The news media are the common carriers of public discussion in much of Africa where political leaders fear and hate it, and this responsibility forms a basis for our special privileges. This discussion serves society best when it is informed by facts rather than prejudice and supposition. It also should strive to fairly represent the varied viewpoints and interests in society, and to place them in context rather than highlight only the conflicting fringes of debate. Accuracy and truthfulness require that as framers of the public discussion we should not neglect the point of common grounds where problem solving occur. In African countries which are so tortured and convulsed by ethnic conflicts, journalists should never be oblivious of this vital role.

5) Employ an Ethical Method of Verification

Journalists rely on a professional discipline for verifying information. When the concept "objectivity" originally evolved, it did not imply that journalists are free of bias. It called, rather, for a consistent method of testing information - a transparent approach of evidence - precisely so that personal and cultural biases would not undermine the accuracy of their work. The method is objective, not the journalist. Seeking out multiple witnesses, disclosing as much as possible about sources or asking various sides for comments, all signals such standards. This discipline of verification is what separates journalism from other modes of communication, such as propaganda, fiction or entertainment. But the need for the professional method is not always fully recognized or refined. While journalism has developed various techniques for determining facts, for instance, it has done less to develop a system for the reliability of journalistic interpretation. This phenomenon is pervasive in Francophone Africa where only "hallelujah" singing assures a journalist of promotions or even being associated with journalism.

6) Maintain Independence from Factional/Fractional Politics.

Independence is an underlying requirement of journalism, a cornerstone of reliability.

Independence of spirit and mind, rather than neutrality, is the principle journalists must keep in focus. While editorialists and commentators are not neutral, the source of their credibility is still accuracy, intellectual fairness and ability to inform - not their devotion to a certain group or outcome. In our independence, however, we must avoid any tendency to stray into arrogance, elitism, isolation or nihilism.

7) Make the News Engaging and Relevant

Journalism is story- telling with a purpose. It should do more than gather an audience or catalogue the important. For its own survival, it must balance what readers know they want with what they cannot anticipate but need. In short, it must strive to make the significant interesting and relevant. Quality must be measured with how much a work engages its audience and enlightens it. This means journalists must continually ask what information has most value to citizens and in what form. While journalism should reach beyond such topics as government and public safety, a journalist overwhelmed by reeve and false significance ultimately engenders a trivial society.

8) Keep News Comprehensive and proportional

Keeping news in proportion and not leaving important things out are also cornerstones of truthfulness. We are stressing this point because of the way some journalists tend to select only what their masters want to hear instead of that which is truthful and comprehensive. Journalism is a form of cartography: It creates a map for citizens to navigate society. Inflating events for sensation, neglecting others, stereotyping or being disproportionately negative all make a less reliable map. The map also should include news of all our communities, not just those with attractive financial handouts and demographics. This is best achieved by newsrooms with a diversity of backgrounds and perspectives. The map is only an analogy; proportion and comprehensiveness are subjective, yet their elusiveness does no lesson their significance.

9) Remain True to personal Conscience

Every journalist must have a personal sense of ethics and responsibility - a moral compass. Each of us must be willing, if fairness and accuracy require, to voice differences with our colleagues, whether in the newsroom or the executive suite. News organizations do well to nurture this independence by encouraging individuals to speak their minds. This stimulates the intellectual diversity necessary to understand and accurately cover an increasingly diverse society. It is this diversity of minds and voices, not just numbers that matters. . A newsroom filled with spies for an insecure regime is a real danger to democracy and the profession itself.

To live effectively is to live with adequate information, the old saying goes. The instruments of social communication or what is commonly called Press is the bellwether of freedom of speech by its very concept. Freedom of the Press consequently becomes only one species of a larger genus-freedom of expression. With this in mind, it is understood that freedom of the press refers to the absence of restraints upon the ability of individuals, or groups, to communicate their ideas to others, subject to the understanding that they do not in their own turn exert pressure on others into paying attention or that they do not invade other rights essential to the dignity of the individual.

The picture to this freedom of the press is being mottled, being shiny and bright in some places in Africa (like Nigeria) and dull and faded in others (like Equatorial Guinea where there is no thought of a private newspaper whatsoever). In fact, some African countries have had consistently notorious records of press suppression. By way of quixotic governmental control through censorship, intimidation, government control of newsprint and veiled threats, some African rulers have created a "kept press" which is one of Africa's post-independence creations. In most states, the banner of press freedom has risen and fallen in the indecisive surging of political events as draconian dictators come and go. The toll on the credibility of the Press in Africa is great. And its future continues to be bleak. We are reminded of Emperor Bokassa of Central Africa who would walk into the Radio or Television studio and give an "erring" child (journalist) a snake beating and suspend him from going near the microphone.

Africa's Press which barked with an awesome bite and raised hell against western imperialists and their exploitative and repressive tactics has been muted by ironbound government and financial restrictions. Both African and World opinion has become increasingly and inescapably critical of this prickly situation. Does Press Freedom in Africa mean merely chanting anti-imperialist and anti-racist slogans? Or does it simply mean glorifying Africa's "Kings" like the "Conqueror of the British Empire"?

The contemporary African Press has been deprived of their expected and normal social processes through which people can exchange meanings bearing reciprocal effects upon each other's behaviour. And, by this means, the Press can authoritatively reinstate the sanctity of human rights. This deprivation is bi-dimensional. The Press has not only been excluded from their social group (with its consequent loss of social relationship), but has also been denied its appropriate social performance or set of relationships. The Press has been allotted a lower social status than it is clearly suitable for it. In other words, Africa's Press has been rejected and even relegated to mere speech-links, to poet laureates of the status quo.

In effect, the African Press has both been denied its necessary social responsibility towards the entire continent in particular and towards humanity in general. It has also been stripped naked of its adult status, and it is now like a child, not greatly loved and accepted, but rejected, deprived of its much-needed and normal social interaction. In the Federal Republic of Nigeria, could one imagine a journalist who has the guts to criticise General Sani Abacha? Where are the Ken Saro Wiwas?

The African Press is the more frustrated by its external counter-parts. When the African Press attempts to enlighten Africans about the evils of neo-colonists and their agents (their only safe area of influence), the messages are vigorously countered by imperialist-controlled media and publicity agencies which have developed sophisticated techniques of bare-faced deception.

Clapped between active bloody politics as experienced in some African dictatorships accompanied by zealous demands for euphemistic official prose to placate mass misery and social inertia, and dwarfed by weak economic means, the African Press has sacrificed its Conscience politics for worthless self-preservation. Africa's contemporary Press now stands like a league of frightened men – men freezing helplessly in a fridge of fear and poverty and only a very raw animal courage could be necessary to get them out. A glowing example is that of the Publisher of the monthly magazine *Jeune Afrique Economie* who was chased out of Yaoundé, Cameroon, because of an interview he had with the Archbishop of Douala, Christian Cardinal Tumi. The Cardinal, in the interview, disclosed some demonic acts of the Biya regime such as killing people and dumping their corpses in mass graves in Douala, during the murderous period of *Commandement Operationnel* in the early 1990s. All these revelations by the Cardinal were true as demonstrated by the corpses found in mass graves in **La Foret des Singes** in **Douala**.

But, *The Herald* newspaper, which was militantly seeking government favours came out to mock at the Cardinal in an editorial titled "Yaoundé has last laugh on Tumi". Nobody can tell what such a newspaper may say since it is apparently not yet schooled enough to understand that Cameroonians have lived, and are still living, an epoch where telling lies has become the cornerstone of government policy. This brand of opportunistic journalism is noteworthy because multiple examples of this nature toll on the integrity of the Press. And such performance of the Press has reached a point of near irreversible distrust. What a contrast? Are these not the very instruments of social communication which raised anti-colonial consciousness in Africans? Are they not the very weapons which shattered ageless, heavily armed western anti-independence struggles in Africa exemplified by Dr. Nnamdi Azikiwe's press network which earned him the name the "giant of journalism in Africa"? Why are these instruments of social communication now instead playing a spoiling role in a job they started so forcefully, effectively and successfully?

Selected Bibliography

Bay, Christian. *The Structure of Freedom*, Stanford: Stanford University Press, 1970.

Calm, Edmond. *The Moral Decision*, (Bloomington: Indiana University Press, 1956.

Chafee, Zechariah, Jr., *Government and Mass Communication*: Vol. 142; A Report from the Commission on Freedom of the Press (Chicago: University of Chicago Press, 1947).

Christian, S., Clifford G; Rotzoll, Lim B; and Fackler, Mark. *Media Ethics, Cases and Moral Reasoning* (New York and London: Longman, 1983).

Friedrich, Carl J. *The Philosophy of Kant.* (New York: Random House, 1949).

Gaux, Gerald F. *The Modern Liberal Theory of Man,* (Mew York: St Martin's Press, 1983).

Rivers, William L; and Schramm, Wilbur. *Responsibility in Mass Communication,* (New York: Harper and Row, 1969).

Schaeffer, David Lewis: *Justice or Tyranny? A Critique of John Rawls' Theory of Justice,* (Port Washington, N.Y Kennikat Press, 1969).

Siebert, Fred S.; Peterson Theodore; and Schramm, Wilbur. *Four Theories of the Press)* (Urbana: University of Illinois Press 1963).

Sobel, Lester A. *Media Controversies.* (New York: Facts on file, 1981).

Spragens, Thomas A. Jr *The Irony of Liberal Reason* (Chicago and London: Univ. of Chicago Press 1981).

Thayer, Lee: *Ethics, Morality and the Media,* (New York: Hastings House 1980).

Thiroux, Jacques P. *Ethics, Theory and Practice* 2nd Ed. : (Encino, Calif: Glencoe Publishing 1980).